PRESENTED TO

To:

From:

The Spirit without Borders

A Christian's Guild to Self-Publishing

Robin Bremer

The Spirit without Borders

A Christian's Guide to Self-Publishing

ISBN-13: 978-1496014603

ISBN-10: 149601460X

DEDICATION

This book is dedication to the freedom of the Holy Spirit. I pray that every Christian that has a testimony, teaching, gifts, callings and talents uses this book to set others free, and to demonstrate the power and goodness of God.

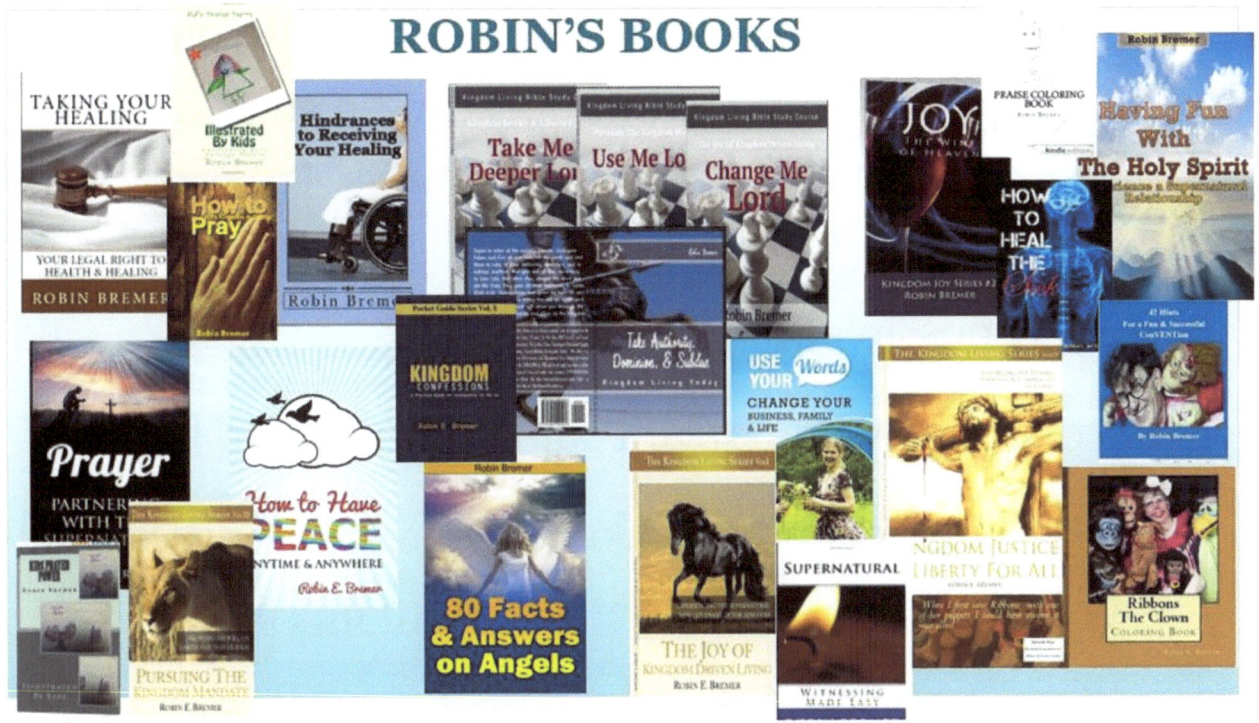

Congratulations on writing your book! I hope to make self-publishing easy for you through pictures and charts. I self-published my first book at the cost of $1,500. Then I was blessed that a publisher picked it up and published it. However, the publisher soon went out of business but not before they taught me how to use Amazon (Createspace) to self-publish my future books. Read through this whole book before you begin, to determine at what point would be the most helpful for where you are currently at on your book writing project.

My purpose in writing this book is so that your gifts, calling, talents and testimonies can be shared with others through the medium of a book. I have tried to keep this book simple and to the point to make it as easy as possible for you to succeed.

Here are a few important things you should know.

The average chapter is around 10 pages long (It can be much longer but not is better not to be shorter).

You should have a few important people read your manuscript ASAP once it is edited so they can have **time to read it** (a few months works good for a 100 page book) and **give you an endorsement** to publish in the book and use for other publicity purposes. PLEASE send them a reminder to read your book and THE DEADLINE you want them to send you the endorsement.

To make things easier check off projects as you do them.

Createspace's **LEAST amount of pages** they will publish **is 24**. So make sure it has at least that many pages. If it has less you CAN publish it as an eBook at

http://www.Smashwords.com for free and give it away or sell it.

Or at https://kdp.amazon.com/self-publishing

After you FINISH the main part of your book or when you are almost done you can do the following things.

1. _____ **Create a folder** on your computer to put all your book info in so it is easily accessible. I suggest you call it "MyBook" folder so you can REMEMBER what you called it!

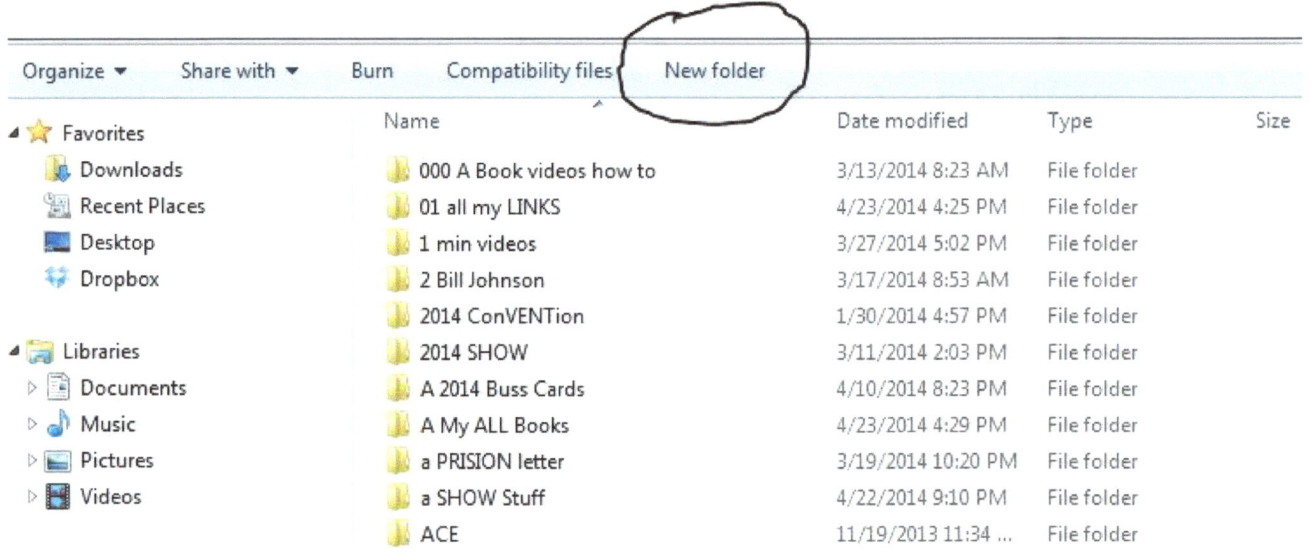

a. You will store endorsements here when they arrive.

b. You will store edited versions of your book here.

c. You will store your template here.

d. You will store your book cover here.

e. Author pictures will go here too.

2. _____**Create a "Word doc"** (or you could also do this in Wordpad or Note) on **your computer** to paste information onto. I suggest you call it, "My_book_info" doc.

   a. You will paste, links, ISBN #, Titles, sub titles, back cover information, and LOTS more.

   b. HERE ARE SAMPLE PICTURES OF WHAT TO STORE IN

My Book Information *(all in one place so that I can copy it and paste it when I need it)*

Title: My title goes here
Subtitle: My subtitle goes here
Page number: 28
Book size: 6x9
Legal stuff:

Page 1

YOUR NEW FILE.

My Author picture

My ISBN:
ISBN-13: 978---4878764 (sample only)
ISBN-10: 14---78763

About the author: ABOUT THE AUTHOR
Robin Bremer is an ordained minister, who has appeared on the Tom Leding TV show "In God Your Will Succeed", and several radio shows. She is also a Comic Ventriloquist Motivational Speaker sharing "Keys to Working the Kingdom System". Her calling is to bring God's presence and Supernatural Power through the message of the KINGDOM of JOY and to set people free from a godless religion of "doing and works" into a personal, SUPERNATURAL relationship with Jesus Christ. Follow Robins' blog http://www.robinbremer.net contact Robin for guest appearances on TV, radio or for speaking engagements at RobinBremer@sbcglobal.net.

ADD YOUR PHONE IS WANTED
Rt 2 Box 1936
Checotah, OK 74426

Other Books by Robin Bremer
Kingdom Living Series Vo. 1-3
Kingdom Living Bible Study Course Vol. 1-3
Pocket Study Guides Vol.1
80 Fact & Answers about Angles
Many e-Books
Dear Friend,
I pray as you read this book your life is changed!
P.S. Make sure you check out my blog:
www.RobinBremer.net
RobinBremer@sbcglobal.net.

5 key words
Christian, end times, family, kids, peace (sample
only)

My links to go in the back of the book.

http://facebook.com/feedmypeoplejoy
http://www.youtube.com/user/feedmypeoplejoy
http://www.twitter.com/feedmypeoplejoy
http://pinterest.com/robinbremer

3. _____Make an account at

http://www.createspace.com

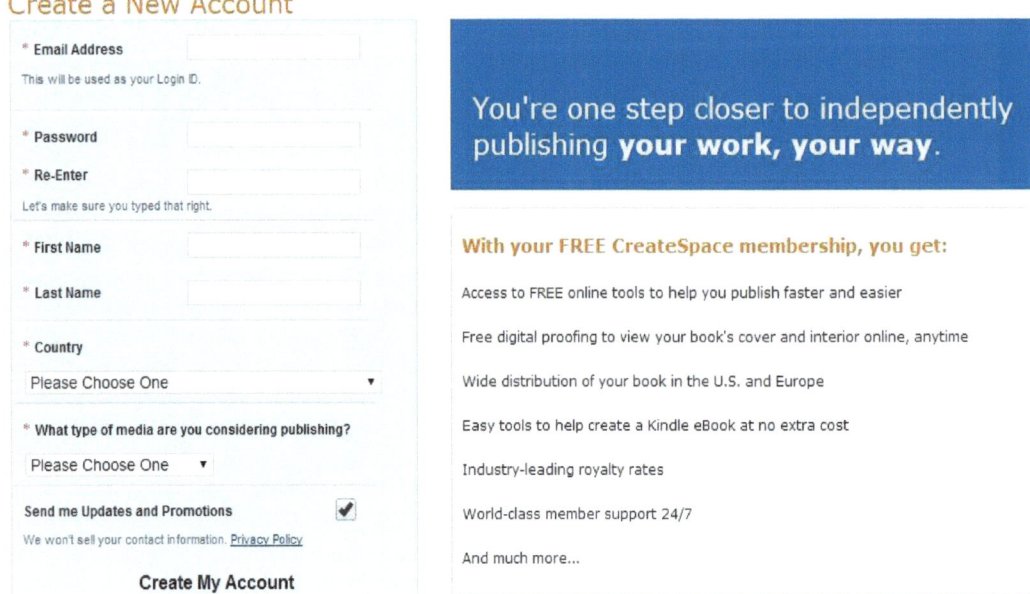

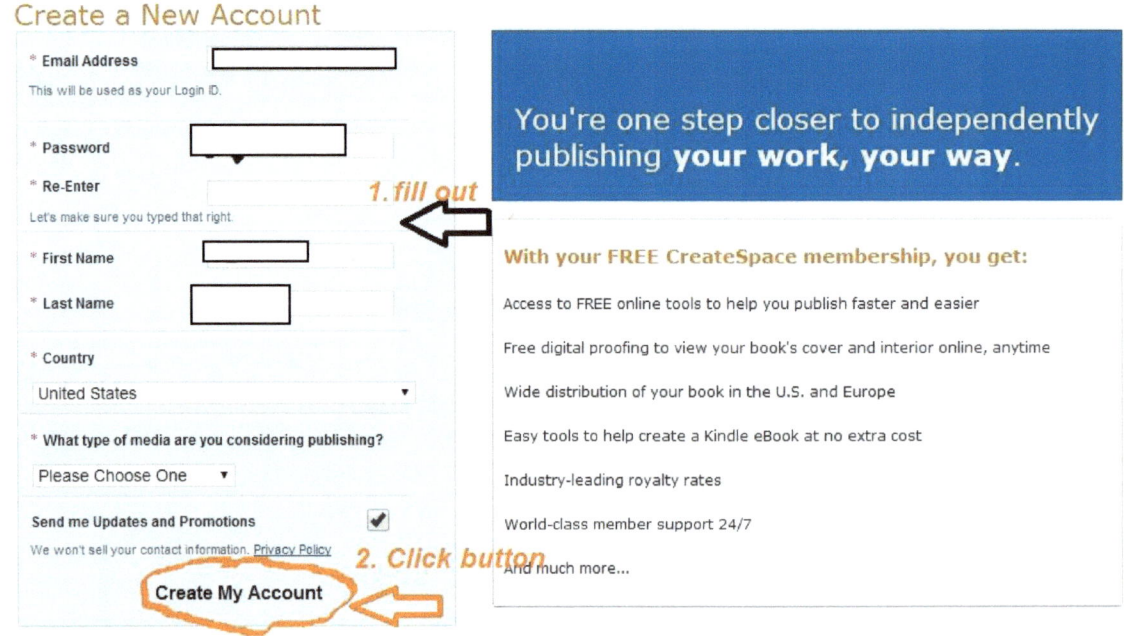

Go to your mail box and open the Welcome letter from "CreateSpace" and click on the confirm link in the letter and it will SKIP THIS picture below and instead take you right to your Member Dashboard.

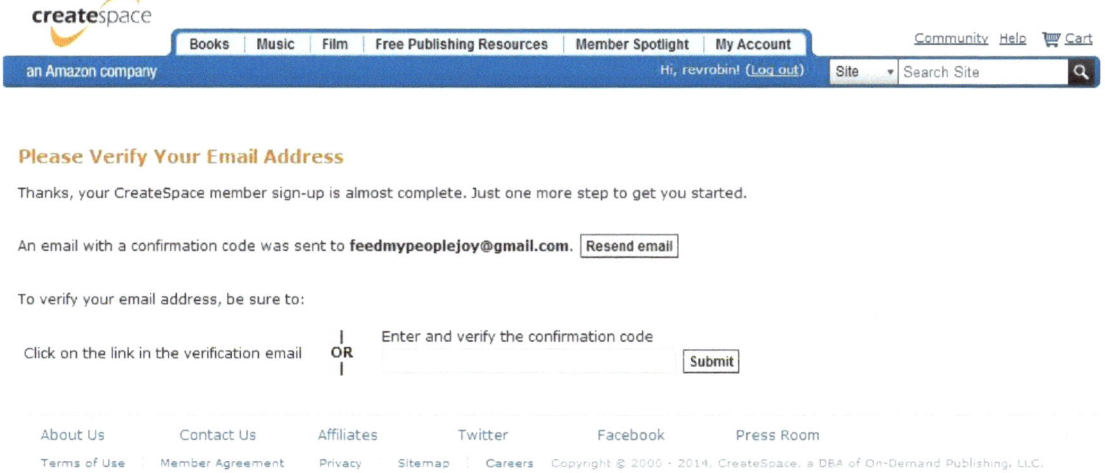

You will end up here.

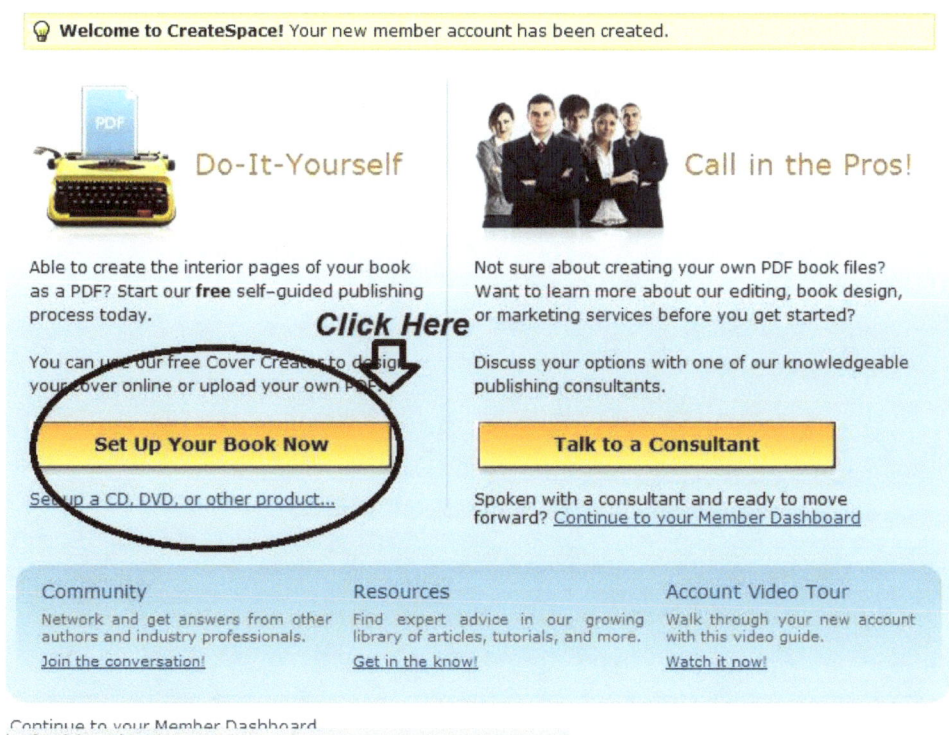

a. Create a title (you can change it later).

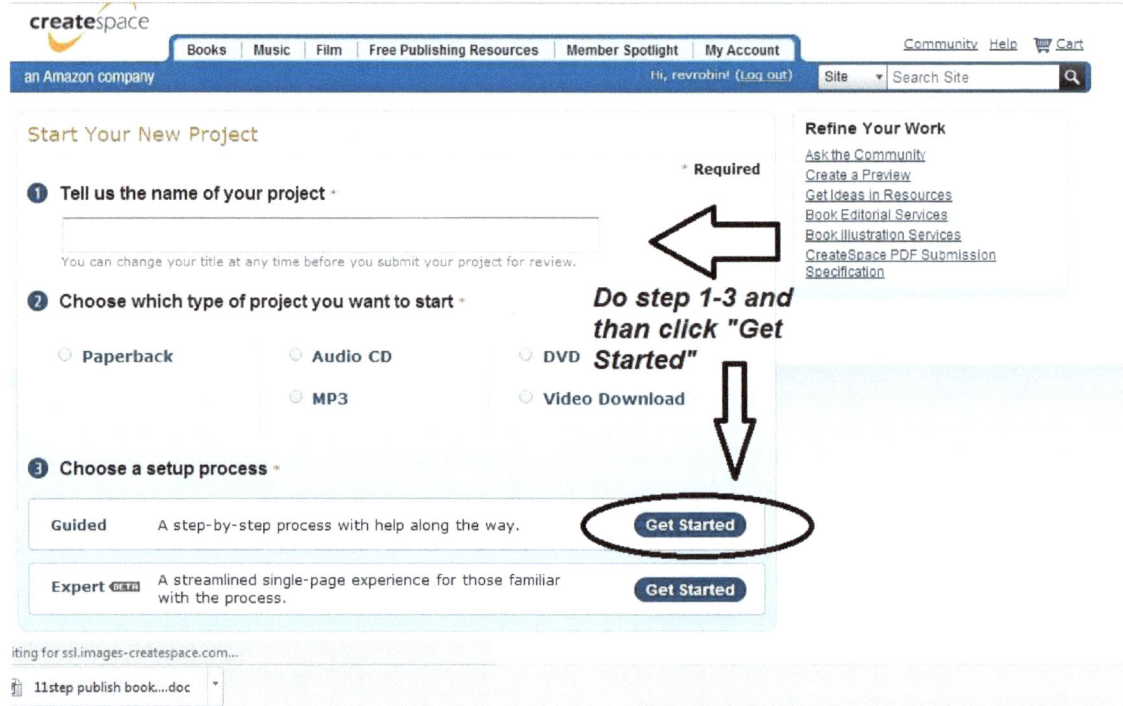

b. Fill out this page and click on the "Save & Continue" blue button at the bottom right of the page.

c. Under "Choose an ISBN option for your book"
(straight underneath in the middle of the page)
Click on "Free CreateSpace-Assigned ISBN."

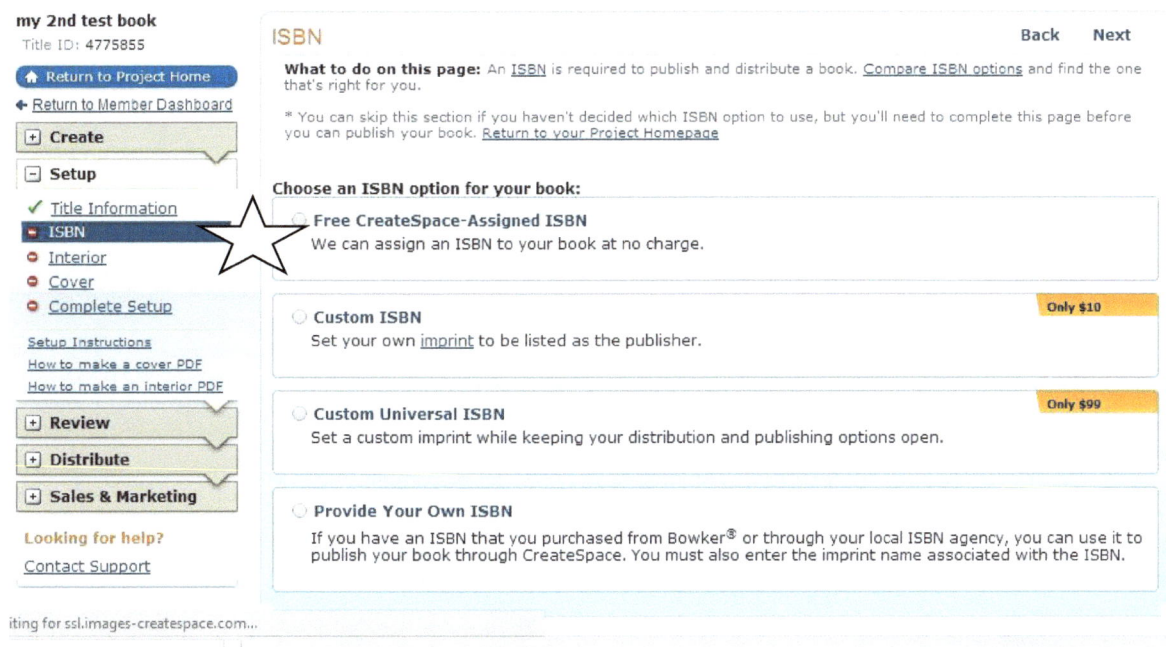

Click on "Assign Free ISBN" in the lower right corner
(the dark blue button).

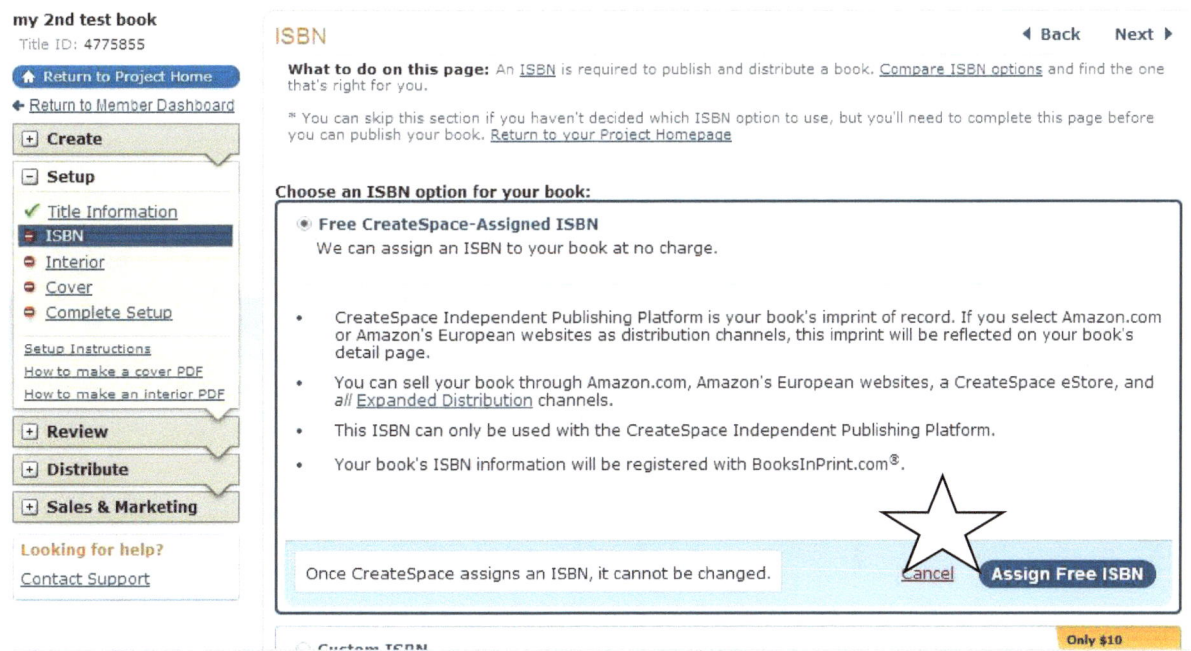

COPY BOTH ISBN NUMBERS

1. Pick your interior type (color or black & white)

2. Pick your color of paper (cream or white)

3. Pick current size or pick a new book size.

If you pick "Choose a different size" you will be taken to the book size picture page. Click on the size you want.

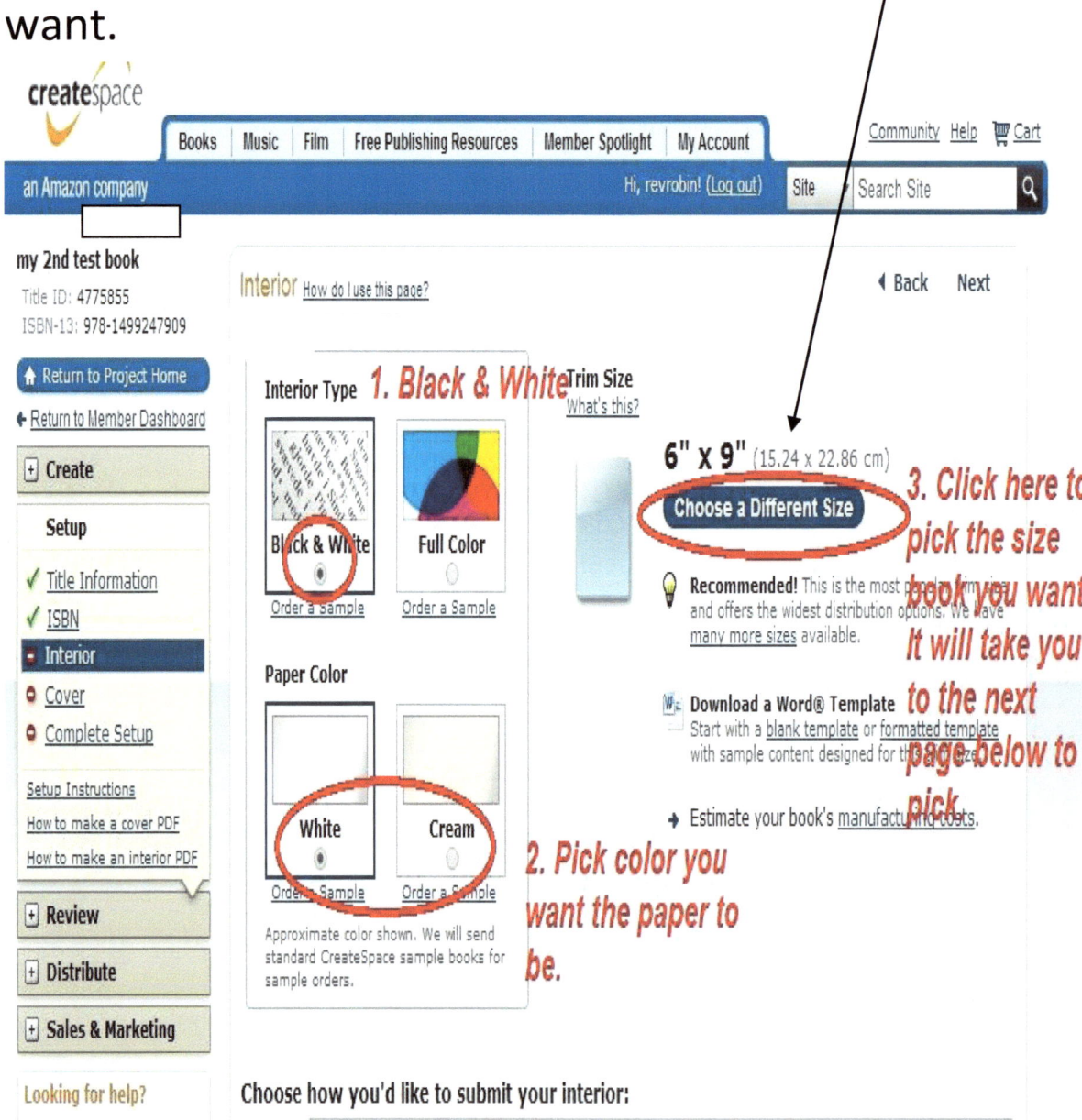

This page will open. **Pick the book size** you want.

Black & White Trim Sizes

close ☒

Most Popular Trim Sizes

5" x 8"
12.7 x 20.32 cm

5.25" x 8"
13.34 x 20.32 cm

5.5" x 8.5"
13.97 x 21.59 cm

6" x 9"
15.24 x 22.86 cm

More Industry-Standard Choices

5.06" x 7.81"
12.85 x 19.84 cm

6.14" x 9.21"
15.6 x 23.39 cm

6.69" x 9.61"
16.99 x 24.41 cm

7" x 10"
17.78 x 25.4 cm

7.44" x 9.69"
18.9 x 24.61 cm

7.5" x 9.25"
19.05 x 23.5 cm

8" x 10"
20.32 x 25.4 cm

8.5" x 11"
21.59 x 27.94 cm

 Compare all sizes to 8.5" x 11" (PDF, 363k)

More Sizes

Click on the size you want to make your book. The fewer pages you have, the smaller the book should be. The page will come up like this:

Under "Download a Word Template", click on
"Formatted Template." To download a template in
the size you want. (You copy and paste your book
interior onto the template.)

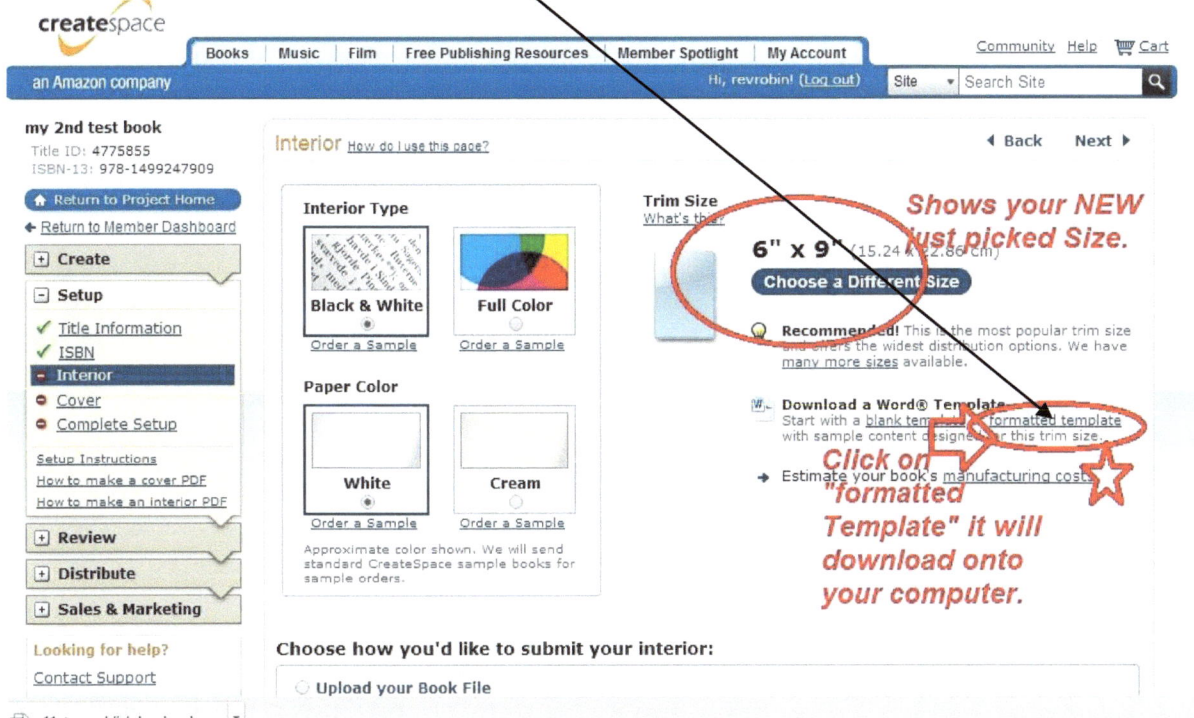

_____ **Download a template for your book size.**

_____ Save your formatted template in your
"My_book_folder".

4. _____ Make an account at

a. **http://www. fiverr.com** (IF you want to pay
someone $15.00 for your book cover, spine and
back.) You can also create your own book cover with
Createspace book cover launcher.

5. _____ Make your **BOOK COVER** at

   a. Pick someone at **http://www.fiverr.com ($15.00) to** make your book cover.(This takes 3 days up to 2 weeks)

   b. **Or pick someone at http://www.Elance.com**

   c. You will need to give them (Whoever makes your cover this information below)

      1. _____ Author info

      2. _____ Author picture

      3. _____ Back of book info.

      4. _____ What size the book will be

      5. _____ Approx. how many pages it will be (it's important to get the pages close to that amount in the finished book). You can add a few blank pages if you need to, or make the print larger.

6. _____ **EDIT your book** file at:

http://www. fiverr.com

http://www.Elance.com (highest prices)

or find 3 friends to edit if for you.

Check for spelling, grammar, sentence structure, and punctuation.

ANYTIME & ANYWHERE

In a world full of unpredictable weather, incurable disease, unfaithfulness and mixed up standards of what is right and wrong, how can anyone have peace and confidence? There is only one way to have peace in all situations and circumstances and that is through the unconditional love and undeserved supernatural power of knowing and experiencing God as Your Daddy.

This book will show you that through the unconditional love of God you will have supernatural power to change any circumstances and situations. Fear is false evidence that appears real. Peace is knowing an all-loving God who has given to you everything you need to live on earth like you will in heaven.

Learn about your Daddy's love and power toward you and for you and walk in power and peace.

Robin E. Bremer is an ordained minister, which has appeared on the Tom Leding TV show "In God Your Will Succeed", and several radio shows. She is also a Comic Ventriloquist Motivational Speaker sharing "Keys to Working the Kingdom System". Her calling is to bring God's presence and Supernatural Power through the message of the KINGDOM of JOY and to set people free from a godless religion of "doing and works" into a personal, SUPERNATURAL relationship with Jesus Christ. Follow Robins' blog *http://www.robinbremer.net* contact Robin for guest appearances on TV, radio or for speaking engagements at *RobinBremer@sbcglobal.net*.

7. _____ **Make an e-cover** by using Paint (a free and easy-to-use program). You can use the same cover as your print cover, just crop it to only show the Front cover. Make sure you make it the correct size by looking at what they require. This will be the Kindle cover you will use **after you publish your book in Createspace**.

   a.   Or pay someone at http://www. fiverr.com

Kindle Covers

An e-book's cover is only the front and it can be the same as the published version or different.

Putting your book together

This is just one way to put your book together.

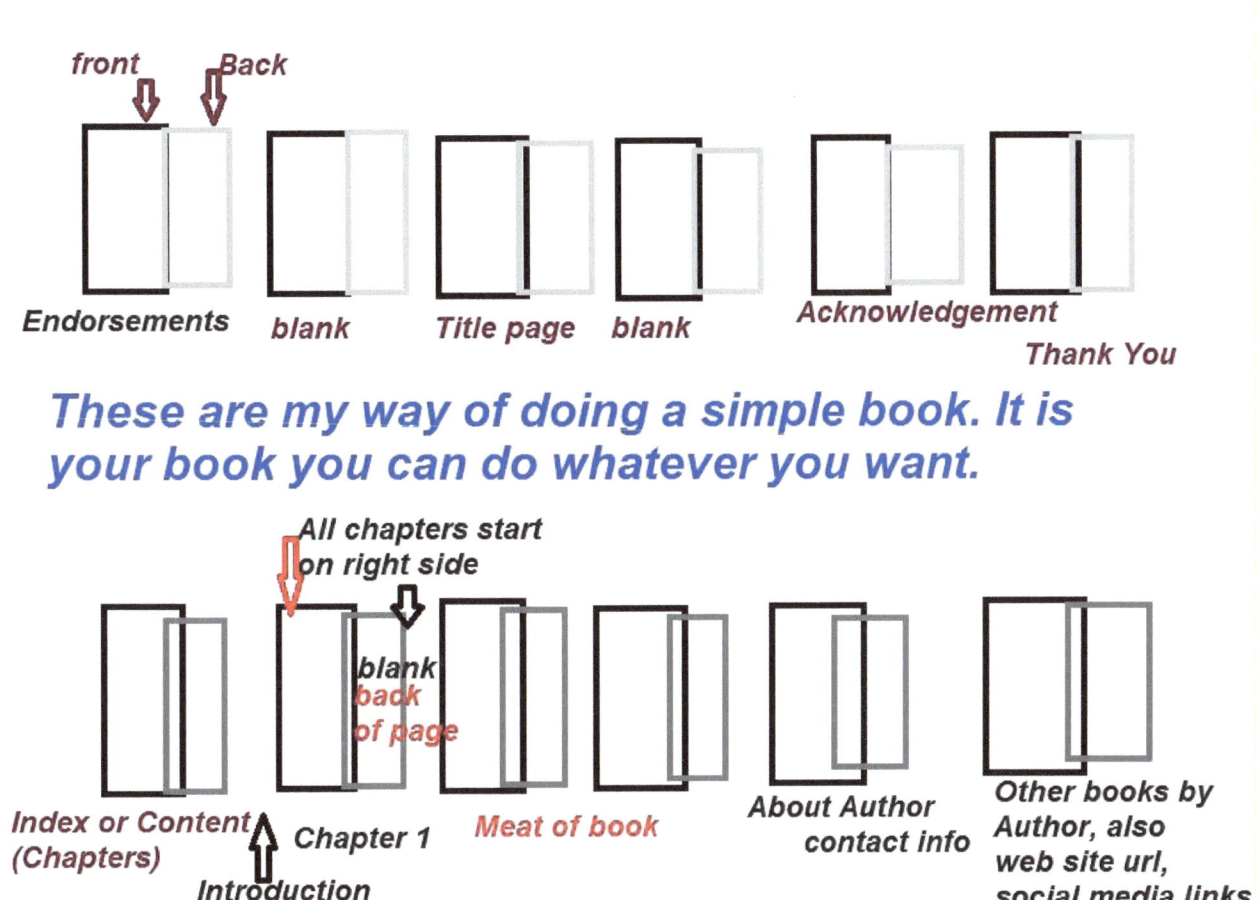

These are my way of doing a simple book. It is your book you can do whatever you want.

Copy information from your "My_book_info" doc, or from the folder I told you to paste info. on to save for future use. Use this chart above to pattern your book after.

a. _____Copy endorsements into book

b. _____Copy ISBN into proper place (on Title page)

c. _____Add "thank you," "acknowledgements," and "Special mentions."

d. _____Add legal copyright info for Bible Scriptures (if it is a Christian book).

e. _____Add legal content front stuff (Also add back stuff: "about author," "Other books by author," "If you like this content Like us on Facebook," etc.)

f. _____Add "Follow us" information & links to Facebook, Web site, Linkedin, Twitter, My Space, You-Tube URL links.

8. PUBLISH AS PRINT BOOK here

a. https://www.createspace.com

b. _____**Create a title on the dashboard or change the Title you created already to get the ISBN number** earlier. Make sure your ISBN is copied into the title page—you can copy it from your Word file.

c. _____Make your book file into a PDF file and submit book file.

d. _____Submit cover files as a PDF file.

e. _____Write short description (store this on your Word Doc till you are ready to copy it).

f. _____Figure out what the "genres" of your book are-example, Christian, cooking, etc.

g. _____Pick 5 keywords.

h. _____Follow their directions to finish page.

i. _____Write author's page.

j. _____Review and revise or submit files for review and after final approval, click publish!

They will copy the book file and cover and make it into a Kindle version after it is all approved and accepted. Then you download it and save it to your computer. If you have finished publishing your book they will say, "Publish on Kindle" click on that button and they will transfer all your information, cover and interior to Kindle.

or

Go to KINDLE:

Go to: https://kdp.amazon.com/

Start an account

Go to bookshelf and submit title

Follow directions

Promote book by copying link (not your own personal link) on all social media sites.

9. _____Set up an "Author's Page" at Amazon

10. _____Set up a Store from Amazon on your blog.

Robinbremer@sbcglobal.net

www.robinbremer.net

If you died tonight do you know where you would go? God sent His Son Jesus to die for you. He paid the price for your past, present and future sins. He paid the price so you could have peace, health, wealth, power and a relationship with Him. Repeat after me: Father God I accept Jesus, thank you that He paid for my sins, be my Lord, show me how much you love me and show me all that Jesus died for me to have. In Jesus' name, amen.

ABOUT THE AUTHOR

Robin Bremer is an ordained minister who has appeared on the Tom Leding TV show "In God You Will Succeed" and several radio shows. She is also a Comic Ventriloquist Motivational Speaker sharing "Keys to Working the Kingdom System." Her calling is to bring God's presence and Supernatural Power through the message of the KINGDOM of JOY and to set people free from a godless religion of "doing and works" into a personal, SUPERNATURAL relationship with Jesus Christ. Follow Robins' blog at http://www.robinbremer.net. You can contact Robin at RobinBremer@sbcglobal.net, or by phone at 918-926-0707.

Robin's Social Media

http://facebook.com/feedmypeoplejoy
http://www.youtube.com/user/feedmypeoplejoy
http://www.twitter.com/feedmypeoplejoy
http://pinterest.com/robinbremer
http://www.linkedin.com/in/robinbremer/

Clowning/Ventriloquist

http://www.gigsalad.com/ribbons_the_clownventriloquist_checotah
http://fiverr.com/ribbonstheclown

Bookstore

http://astore.amazon.com/kinlivforendt-20

Amazon Author's Page

http://www.amazon.com/author/robinbremer

Other Books by Robin Bremer

Print & Kindle

Kingdom Living Series Vo. 1-3
- The Joy of Kingdom Driven Living
- Kingdom Justice & Liberty for All
- Pursuing the Kingdom Mandate

Kingdom Living Bible Study Course Vol. 1-3
- Change Me Lord
- Take Me Deeper Lord
- Use Me Lord

Pocket Study Guides Vol.1
- Kingdom Confessions

The Kingdom Joy Series
- Supernatural Witnessing Made Easy
- Joy, the Wine of Heaven
- Taking Authority, Dominion & Subdue
- Taking Healing: Your Legal Right to Health & Healing
- Hindrances to Receiving Your Healing
- God of Abundance, Overflow & Extravagance

Other Books

80 Fact & Answers about Angels
Use Your Words
42 Hints for a Fun & Successful Convention
How to Have Peace Anywhere Anytime
Prayer, Partnering With the Holy Spirit
Upside Down Love The Unfair Truth About Grace

Children's Books

Ribbons the Clown Coloring Book

Kingdom Kids Series

Praise Party
Kids' Prayer Power

Kingdom Kids Coloring Book Series Praise Coloring book

Audio Books

The Joy of Kingdom Driven Living
Pursuing the Kingdom Mandate

Many e-Books

Dear Pastor & Friends,
I pray as you "do" this book your life is changed! I speak life to your book, it will succeed, it will be promoted and it will bless people's lives. You book IS a blessing and everything you set your hands to do will prosper you.

P.S. Make sure you check out my blog:
www.RobinBremer.net
Check out my books and give me a review.
Contact: RobinBremer@sbcglobal.net.

www.ingramcontent.com/pod-product-compliance
Lightning Source LLC
Chambersburg PA
CBHW060840290526
45792CB00006BB/1995